50 Proven Networking Tips for Career Success

By Shawn K. Lipton

The Trusted Coach, LLC
Seattle, Washington

First Edition

For Nicole and Amelia

Table of Contents

Tip #44: The simpler the better
Tip #45: Summarize the reasons why you are networking
Tip #46: Write down your commitment for the Week
Tip #47: Chunk your goals and set time aside each day
Tip #48: Have a long term plan of action
Tip #49: Have a list of contacts
Tip #50: State why you are connecting and how you will connect

Why Read this Book?

This book focuses on how to build a comprehensive network of professional contacts so you will never have to look for a job the traditional way - sending unsolicited resumes and cover letters or applying to job postings - ever again. If you are currently employed but are starting to think about how you can proactively control your career or are currently looking for a position in a similar or completely different field, then this book is an ideal starting point. This book is focused on career development, methods that will enhance your job search, and techniques that will allow you to have control over your career. It is about career success. If you feel that you need some help in building a solid network of advocates, friends, professional contacts, and business relationships; this book is for you. I will walk you through the key components of developing solid relationships, but more importantly, MAINTAINING them (most of us make connections, but we find it very hard to maintain them – seven tips in a subsequent chapter will focus on methods on how to keep in touch). If I am making sense thus far then let's dive in and I'll introduce a simple definition of networking.

What is Networking?

Some consider it a four letter word, others think of something smarmy or akin to schmoozing. It is nothing of the sort when you approach it genuinely. Yes, networking is about building mutually beneficial relationships; yes, it is about connecting with colleagues in the professional community; and yes, it is about making sure you are established and known in your professional group. That in a nut shell is a way to define networking; however, in my mind, and what I want you to take away from this book is this even simpler definition: **networking is about building relationships whether you need them or not and contributing to the success of others**. I hope that definition resonates with you; it is a critically important point. As we move forward, I will elaborate, but for now, that is all I want you to remember.

Networking: Why Do It

I refuse to bore you with a hundred reasons why I think networking is important. You're already reading this book and likely know how essential networking is to career success. Following are five points that should illustrate the necessity of developing a comprehensive network of contacts.

1. **Information is King.** The more people you meet, (face-to-face), the more information, such as crucial industry trends, you acquire. That information becomes your intellectual property. It gives you a pulse of what's going on in an industry or community. When you have essential information to share, you can see how a relationship quickly becomes mutually beneficial. Stay in the know.

2. **Brainstorming and Sounding Boards.** Two minds are better than one is a cliché, but it also happens to be true. Throwing out ideas, asking questions about next steps, figuring out how best to move forward are all part of the networking process. Networking can lead to great ideas, new strategies, a potential new career path, or a new method to get in front of a decision maker. I had a client, Katherine, who had been on the job hunt for ten months. She had been in finance, but had an undergraduate degree in environmental science and wanted to enter the field of environmental consulting. Katherine had been doing everything right. She joined a local urban planning group, had done an amazing amount of research in the industry, developed the knowledge to be able to confidently enter the field, and was conducting at least one informational interview per week. Unfortunately, none of this led to a job or even an interview. During one of her follow up meetings with a mentor who she originally connected with through an informational interview, she learned of a large contract that was to be granted to her mentor's competitors. The two of them brainstormed how Katherine could differentiate herself and potentially obtain a position from a firm that would most likely be expanding due

to an increase in work. The mentor was invaluable in helping Katherine shape her strategy, but more importantly provided information and the knowledge she needed to really go after this job. Did Katherine obtain the position? You bet she did and utilizing her mentor to help with crafting a plan of attack was crucial.

3. **Encouragement.** Developing your career is hard work and there will be many occasions where you will think the entire process is futile and that is when you can access your network for support. The process of building relationships yields benefits way beyond just finding a job, including relationships with a group of people that are supportive and can encourage you to reach your goals. Your network is a resource that can help take you out of your funk and support you in the process of moving forward with your goals and commitments.

4. **Identify Opportunities Before they Exist.** As anyone reading this knows, the majority of positions never, ever get posted. There is only one way to learn about many opportunities and that is through your network. The individuals you meet may not have a position for you or may not know anyone who is hiring, but by maintaining these contacts, you increase your percentages dramatically that when a position arises in an area of interest, you'll hear about it first. Even if it does get posted, having first mover advantage can be the tipping point you need to land the position.

5. **Be Part of a Community.** I was working with a new attorney who had built a solid network of relationships in the area of labor law, and through her efforts she created a group of cheerleaders that wanted to see her succeed. She was, of course, disappointed that her efforts had not yielded something more tangible, but was happy to have made so many contacts in the industry. She finally saw a job posted online working for a firm in labor law and the same day she saw the job ad, she received four or five e-mails from her contacts encouraging her to apply. She applied for the job and received an interview. When she met the partner of the firm, he said he had been looking forward to the interview

since he had received four calls from attorneys in the community saying how great she was. As you can imagine, she got the job. And, that is what community is all about. When you put yourself out there and connect with people, getting to know them and sharing your interests and passions, they want to help you reach your goals. You can create this community and by nurturing it, by keeping in touch, sharing your own wisdom and, supporting your professional colleagues, you will have created a community that will serve you well in countless ways throughout your professional career.

Commitment & Accountability

You are probably wondering why the very first tip I will describe deals with commitment and accountability. You most likely will not find another networking book in print that will lead with or even address this topic; however, to succeed in creating an effective network of contacts over a career, nothing is more important than your commitment and your accountability to that commitment. You must treat networking as a have-to-have priority in order to achieve long-term career fulfillment, but it is very easy to treat it like a nice-to-have.

One of the problems many of us have is that we have great ideas, but it's just too easy not to pursue them. Personal accomplishment is different from work where if we don't produce, we could be fired or admonished by our boss and it's not like the personal responsibility we have to family or friends. When we have personal goals, the only one holding us accountable is ourselves and at the end of the day, it is pretty easy to blow that off. Yes, when we do not achieve what we initially set out to do, it hurts for a little bit, but once we start thinking about other things, the feeling quickly passes. The problem is that in general, many of us are comfortable in our jobs or with our lives, but we realize that being comfortable is a bit overrated and we want to push ourselves and accomplish more, but breaking out of the comfort mode is not easy. Networking for your professional and career development falls in to that category of personal accountability. There are five ways that I have used to develop accountability and I didn't think initially it would make much difference, but it has.

Tip #1: Find a Mentor/Mentors

An ideal method to develop a sense of accountability is to find a mentor. This will be a person that will understand your goals and provide the support to achieve them. This could be a person in a field of interest or could be someone who you admire or has had success that perhaps you'd like to emulate. Do your due diligence.

You can find a mentor who is speaking at a seminar, someone you read about, or someone you conducted an informational interview with and would like to build a stronger connection. Whatever the case, once you've selected someone, the best way to initially approach the building of the relationship is through an informational interview. You don't want to ask someone to be your mentor when they do not even know you, so take a baby step and try to set up a meeting where you can learn a bit more about them and they can learn about your goals and aspirations. If the initial meeting goes well, the ideal way to make the ask is through a handwritten thank you note. Thank the person for their time and then talk about how much you enjoyed the meeting, how much you learned, and then ask for a more formal mentor/mentee relationship. Leave it short and sweet and most likely the person will come back with specifics about what the expectations may be. Don't make the relationship too much of a burden – perhaps a meeting every few months or an e-mail from time to time with updates. As the relationship develops and matures, you will want to make sure you show how much you appreciate the mentor taking valuable time to guide you in your professional development. Take your time in deciding who may be a good mentor. You may have twenty informational interviews before you find the ideal person. Everyone you meet is a good professional contact, but you'll quickly get a sense of the person with whom you will form a deeper bond. When that happens, make the ask!

Tip #2: Find an Accountability Partner

I don't think there is a better way to assist in the process of holding ourselves accountable than to find someone who can help in the process. Some people are unbelievably disciplined and just do what they set out to do. Some people are driven by fear. But, for the majority of us, we need additional support to help us achieve our goals and that can be found through an accountability partner. The way this works is that you first need to find someone who you think could serve as a motivator – it could be a good friend, a professional colleague you trust, an old classmate, or anyone who will take the task seriously. Avoid all family members. The person should be someone you respect and feel has your best interest at heart. Next, let the person know what you're looking for. Perhaps you want someone to be harsh if you don't achieve what you set out to do or maybe someone who will speak logically about your commitment and tries to understand why you may not be achieving your goals. I personally like someone to be very hard on me. I respect my accountability partner very much and have found when I visualize the prospect of him coming down hard on me about not achieving my goals; it is sufficient motivation. Next, write down your goal and how long it will take you to achieve it. It feels liberating putting it on paper and e-mailing it to your partner. I think you'll find if you approach someone about this idea, they'll be very receptive. Try it out and see if it works.

Tip #3: Take Set Backs in Stride

There will be many networking events that you will plan to attend, but when the time comes, you blow it off. You may get on a roll with informational interviews and then, all of a sudden, stop doing them. You will be disciplined for months on keeping in touch with contacts and recording information in your contact database and then all of a sudden stop doing it. This happens to all of us. We get in a groove, we're moving forward and then something happens – perhaps complacency or discouragement sets in. Maybe we stop for a week and it's hard to get back on the horse, or we're too busy at work, or we get sick, or we go on vacation. It will happen, but the key is to have a recovery plan in place. This can be as simple as recognizing that it happened, genuinely acknowledging that it's ok, not beating yourself up over it, and moving on. The best way is to move forward, but move forward very slowly. Don't look back at all the time lost and say you have to put in double the effort to get back on track. Simply start with a very small task that you know you can achieve in a short period of time and go for it.

In Tip #2, we spoke about an accountability partner. Well, there is one other person in your network that is a necessary component to networking success and that is your cheerleader. In general, I don't think that should be the same person as your accountability partner since that person is generally there to be a bit tough on you. You have set a goal and made a commitment, why aren't you carrying it out? Perhaps you've been doing a ton of relationship building and feel that is has yielded very little or you don't see the cost-benefit. This would make anyone say, "I could be doing other things with my time." This is where it is critical to have a cheerleader. It should be a person close to you, someone you feel comfortable and confident venting to. Invariably, that person will tell you all the great work you have done and all the benefits you've received from connecting with professionals in the community – this conversation should re-energize you and allow you to push through the set back.

Tip #4: *Commit*, I mean really commit to succeed at Networking

You have to elevate networking from a nice-to-have to a have-to-have. This means that you have to link the reasons for networking with your short and long term professional and life goals. Have you thought about those or written them down? If not, do it! If you are not clear on this, before you go full fledged into building relationships, take some time to self-assess what's important and write down some goals for your professional development. You don't have to have an exact place where you want to be. Your goal could simply be to learn more about a certain field, or meet the necessary people to position yourself for a certain type of job, or to learn what you are truly interested in, or to find a new job. Once you link networking to your career development goals, you can make a true commitment based on what you want to accomplish in your life. Once you have written something down (it does not need to be a novel; a short, succinct paragraph will suffice), then you need to really visualize the connection. By taking steps to connect with people and build relationships, you will be able to move closer to your career development goals.

Tip #5: Think very big, but start very small: Chunk your Goals

We all have goals. We set plans for the future, but invariably, a good many of us will never take the first step. Not because we are not smart, or that we don't work hard, or that we don't want it (well, maybe we don't want it bad enough, but more on that later.). We don't accomplish our goals because they are usually so overwhelming that we get paralyzed by the enormity of the task –

it's too much to get our arms around and it just becomes easier to do nothing or maintain the status quo. I went through this to the Nth degree in writing this book. I finally broke through my fear of the monumental task in front of me and the inertia it brought by using two methods: finding an accountability partner and **chunking** my goals. Chunking or breaking down goals in to their smallest parts allowing you to have small wins and achievements is not something I came up with on my own. It is a widely recommended method and many of you have probably seen the tip before, but I can tell you it worked for me and many of my clients. My epiphany came when I was working for Seattle University in 2009. The university was building a new library and every day on the way to my office, I would walk by the construction site. At first, I saw no real progress. Yes, there was dirt moved around and some concrete poured, but nothing of significance. But, little by little the new building began to take shape and as one year passed, the new library was 90% finished. It was a massive project, but daily progress led to what I was seeing before my eyes in late June 2010. I used it as a catalyst and committed to that day-to-day progress and before I knew it, first 4, then 10, then 25 pages were done and lo and behold, by the end of that summer I had almost completed the first draft of this book. It felt great, and I did it by simply starting very small. I committed to writing one page every night, Sunday through Thursday. Sometimes I would get on a role and do close to two pages, but never less than one, and usually, once that one page was done, I turned off the computer and was done. I had accomplished my goal – it was a win! I was easy on myself and wasn't concerned about the quality of writing at the time. I knew once I got on a role, the momentum would carry me forward and there would be time for editing later. I just set one criteria – WRITE!

Another technique that I have found worked well was that I bought a kitchen timer, put it on my desk, and would set it for 30 minutes. Until that timer went off, I would write, write, and write. I don't know why such a simple commitment to write for those 30 minutes worked, but it did. So, start very small, set very achievable goals, and day-by-day you'll be making progress and after a month (yes, in just 30 short, short days), you will have accomplished a lot. You will have developed a very good habit, and you'll be in the zone and unable to stop your forward progress.

Tip #6: Taking Action and My favorite Quote

"Until one is committed, there is hesitancy, the chance to draw back, always ineffectiveness.

Concerning all acts of initiative there is one elementary truth, the ignorance of which kills countless ideas and splendid plans; that the moment one definitely commits oneself, then providence moves too.

All sorts of things occur to help one that would never otherwise have occurred. A whole stream of events issues from the decision, raising in one's favor all manner of unforeseen incidents and meetings and material assistance, which no man could have dreamed would have come his way.

Whatever you can do or dream you can do
Begin it
Boldness has genius, power, and magic in it
Begin it Now."

Goethe

Take this quote and make it your own or find one that works well for you. Tape it to your computer screen so every night it's the last thing you read when you log off and the first thing you read in the morning or tape it to your bathroom mirror which can have an even more dramatic effect (Your significant other may think you're a bit weird. Mine did!). This quote has the power to impact your life. I know, I know, at this point, you probably think I'm a bit crazy, but take my word for it with this one, and read and re-read this quote, embrace it and live by it. It has worked wonders for my motivation levels and has kept me focused. Try it!

Building your Contact list and Methods to Connect

You are set to go and ready to connect, but who to connect with? Many will say I don't know anyone nor have the time to invest into developing relationships. It is hard work, but there are methods that will make it easier.

In implementing the tips that follow, an introductory e-mail generally will be effective to establish an initial contact. Keep it short and professional. In the subject line mention how you identified the person - name the person who suggested you connect, site the article you read, or say if it was from twitter, or a blog, or try to be creative; something that will spark the person's interest. In the body of the e-mail, elaborate on the connection and ask for fifteen minutes of the person's time to pick their brain. At the end of the 50 tips is a sample e-mail. In Tip #25 we will talk about how to use a hard-copy letter as an alternative method if e-mail is not appropriate or is not working.

Tip #7: A Face-to-Face Meeting is Critical

Your goal is always, always, always to get in front of the person for an informational interview. These interviews are not over-rated, they lead to opportunities. If you are talking to someone at an event and exchange cards, you must follow up (e-mail is best) the very next day so you are still in the person's mind. A connection can be established at an event and potentially be maintained through e-mail, but the only way a solid, professional, trusting relationship can be built is through one-on-one contact and that initial follow up and first meeting are absolutely critical. If you even wait one week and try to re-connect, the possibility of getting that follow up meeting greatly diminishes. It's important to pounce right after the event, when the conversation is still fresh in the person's mind. Once you have the first meeting, a relationship can grow. In an ideal world, you will try to have coffee every six months or so, but in many cases, you'll maintain your connection through e-mail, serendipitous meetings, and association events and that is perfectly fine and works extremely well. But, you can't get to the point where e-mail and chance encounters are effective until you've had the face-to-face and spent some time connecting, finding common ground, and establishing that you both feel this could be a mutually beneficial relationship. **That meeting has to happen.**

Tip #8: Connect with everyone you already know

Most people do not realize how many people they already know and who their family members and friends know. What I suggest as a first step is to write down everyone who may be a good contact or at least worth a conversation. Really put pen to paper here and **just start making a list**. This could be old friends from school, professors from university, or old family friends. At this first step, do not worry about whether this person can potentially help in your career development, just make as comprehensive of a list as possible. Later, you can set up a system where you list the importance of each contact and can actually make a priority list. In making this list, throw the net far and wide. Tell close friends and family that you are starting to think about next steps, (if you are currently in the heart of a job search they will, obviously, already know) and ask them if they can think of anyone who could provide insight. Again, at this point, do not dismiss any name out of hand. It's easy to say, "that person can't help", but you just never know.

I was working with a client, Katelyn, who wanted to take her health insurance sales experience and change career paths and do online media sales. Katelyn had been actively looking to change for close to a year and her search was getting a bit frustrating. She was a good networker, but was also reticent about stretching her contact base beyond close contacts and professional colleagues. After an initial discussion, she did exactly what I had mentioned above and included any name possible on her list. Everyone she spoke to, she let know in specific terms what she was looking for. One person she had on her list was someone she had met at the gym a few years ago and would run into maybe once a month. They were friendly, but had never had more than a few minute conversation. But, the next time Katelyn saw this person, she mentioned that she was in the job hunt and what do you know, the person provided a name of a friend who had just gotten a position in online media sales. That person in turn connected her with a headhunter that she had used, and after a number of months, that headhunter helped find Katelyn a position. This 'gym friend' would never have been someone she would consider as a professional colleague, but she threw it out there in a very non-committal way and the person offered to help. People are willing to help, but if you don't open yourself up to receiving the help, you are not even putting yourself in the hunt.

After you have created an exhaustive list, you can then separate people in to categories. I like to break it down in to three easy groups. A 'have-to-have' group of contacts that is absolutely essential that you meet with. People in this group may be already established in their chosen field, folks that are generally well connected in the community, or individuals that you know will have great ideas to move forward and are a source of insight and encouragement. The second category is the 'nice-to-haves'. This group is similar to the first, but just maybe not quite as good in terms of status in the industry or presence in the community. These two categories may be tough to separate, but it's good to think about it since you want to make sure you are using your time as efficiently as possible. I would still put the 'nice-to haves' in the important to contact category. The third and final group is the 'contact later' group. This is also an important group since as you should now know from reading this tip, every contact is a good contact. You never know who will be the diamond in the rough and provide the connection that you have been waiting for, but it is also good to prioritize and to not feel overwhelmed with the task. If there are some people you just don't have time to get to right away, put them in this group, but make sure you do get to this group. It's not a no pile, but simply a pile that you can delay contacting. When you're parsing through the list, there may be a couple of names (most likely not many) that probably aren't worth your time. At this point, when organizing your comprehensive list, you can drop a few names.

After you have set up these categories, I like to tag each one with 'Difficult to contact', 'Doable', and 'Easy'. It's extremely important to do this since building relationships is hard work and burn-out will happen if you don't make sure that you're getting some small wins along the way.

After you have done this considerable amount of work, you will be well on your way to having an amazing network of people that will want to help you and support you as you build your career. But, there are other methods to identify potential contacts.

Tip #9: Utilize Google Alerts

This is one of the best and easiest methods to stay on top of industry related stories around the country and world. I highly recommend you set up a Google Alert. Go to Google.com and type in Google Alerts – the directions are easy to follow. You can follow an industry, an individual, or see what specific companies are doing. It's an absolutely amazing resource and helps you to avoid information overload. For me, I like to stay up to date on issues involving career development, so my key words are "career development" and "job search". You can choose how often you would like to receive the feed and I recommend not more than once per day, since it will become difficult to keep up and will defeat the purpose of trying to control the amount of information you need to comb through in order to find something pertinent. Each evening, I look through the list of links quickly and if I identify something interesting, I'll click on the link. I set a limit of twenty minutes for this each night. Since career development happens to be a topic I am very interested in, it's easy to spend too much time just reading articles thus there is the risk that a process which helps keeps me informed, has the potential to become counter-productive. As you can imagine, this is an easy, efficient, and effective way of identifying contacts in your field or industry of interest. It will allow you to tailor your correspondence when trying to obtain a meeting with a potential contact. Once you meet, you'll have a good sense of their background and be able to talk about their work and the industry in an intelligent way leading to a much more productive meeting/informational interview and portraying what will likely be a much more favorable impression to perhaps a future boss, mentor, or professional colleague. Not to mention, the alerts also provide plenty of information allowing you to hold your own at industry gatherings and networking events.

Tip #10: Follow Blogs and Tweeters Strategically

Blogs and Twitter feeds can also be a valuable source of information, but as the title of this tip suggests, you want to use these methods strategically, since there is a threat of the law of diminishing marginal returns where information is great until the point where it's overwhelming. That said, it's a very good idea to start following a few blogs and Twitter feeds in a couple of fields you are interested in. Almost on a daily basis someone will be mentioned that would be a good contact to add to your list. More importantly, members of the industry will also follow some of the top blogs and Twitter feeds and many will comment, so this is another way to get names of people in the industry. I would also suggest you begin tweeting yourself (see Tip #17 below). In many cases, to start you may be simply retweeting interesting information, but if people think the content you are sharing is valuable, you will start developing a following. A blog, of course, is also a good idea, but takes great commitment. If you have the time and the knowledge to share, go for it, but remember, no one likes a stale blog.

Tip #11: Do you know anyone else I can talk to

If you remember anything from this book, this is the tip to etch in your mind (well, there are other really good ones as well. Ok, they're all good, but this one is excellent :)). Whenever you have an informational interview, the last question you always have to ask is: "Thank you for your time, I really appreciate it. As I continue to gain knowledge, I am looking to talk to and connect with as many people as possible, do you know anyone else I may be able to talk to?" Unless the informational interview went horribly wrong which if you've prepared, most likely won't happen, this has to be how you end every single informational interview. It is the most important question you will ask. If you get just one or two names from everyone you connect with, you will have covered some very good ground quickly. Moreover, putting a familiar name at the top of a letter or in the subject line of an e-mail (always confirm with the person that this is ok) will almost guarantee that you get a response. The other big reason to do this is that it gives you a tangible and concrete action item from the meeting. Informational interviews are undeniably effective simply from an informational perspective, but they are very much a soft sell approach to career development so after doing many of these, burnout is a possibility. At times, after many informational interviews, you'll ask, "what's next". Of course, the theme of this book is to build relationships for the long term, so every connection is a good one, but it's natural to get frustrated when you don't feel like you are moving forward especially if you have been out of work or are anxious to move on. In order to avoid this feeling, it's nice to have a concrete take-away. By getting a contact or two, you have received something tangible and it gives you a solid next step in the process. No matter what, make sure you ask.

Tip #12: Book of Lists

Most major cities across the country have a business journal that produces a yearly book containing the list of major companies, law firms, non-profits, public companies, private companies, largest companies, (you get the picture) in your area. At the time of publication, there were 68 cities with a book of lists. The following link takes you to additional information and a way to purchase the book for your city of interest. http://www.bizjournals.com/bookoflists/. Alternatively, every library should have this book in their reference section so it should be quite easy to tap this resource for free. The larger companies and especially the publically traded companies are quite easy to identify, but the majority of hiring across the country happens in smaller companies and this is where the Book of Lists really proves its worth. It will list the largest private companies, many of which you have never heard of, but equally important, it lists the top companies in a variety of industries, including environmental consulting, public relations firms, graphic design firms, advertising agencies, and many others. From the list, you can get to the website and start doing additional research to learn more about the company. Let's say your goal is to target larger companies – the difficulty with that is that the people listed on the website are usually the senior officers and most likely will not have the time to meet for informational interviews. It's enticing to think that if you write a compelling letter, that you may get a bite, but the cost benefit simply does not add up. You want to connect with the managers of various groups within a department – people that are making hiring decisions and are focused on strategy, but are not so senior that the likelihood of getting a bite is greatly diminished. The Book of Lists will help you identify the companies and through Google Alerts or LinkedIn, you may just be able to identify the decision makers who will listen to your pitch. Your contact list will grow dramatically and your research will be much more productive by using this resource.

Tip #13: Industry publications

An excellent way to identify contacts is through industry publications. Almost every field you can think of will have their own publication and many local associations will have a quarterly journal as well as online publications. It's important to stay up to date on these journals and track not only people who are mentioned in articles, but also make sure to take note of the authors and advertisements. Industry publications can also be used strategically to establish yourself as a person with knowledge in that you can submit an article for publication (more on how to do that later in the book), comment on an article with a letter to the editor, or if online, add commentary and join the discussion of a particular article that you found interesting. In many industry publications, a good amount of the articles will be written not by full time journalists, but by members of the community who are potential connections. If you liked the article, reach out to the author and share your thoughts directly and propose a meeting to learn more. Any author is flattered that someone is actually reading what they invariably spent a lot of time and effort producing, so the likelihood of you getting an affirmative response is pretty good. You will not be the only person to reach out to the author, but if you **persist**, a meeting is inevitable.

Tip #14: Associations, Alumni functions, and Networking Events

Associations are a good way to connect with people. Consistency is key. Choose one or two groups or associations and get involved. Volunteer to work the registration table, show up early, do your research on the speaker, etc. Really commit to be a contributing member of this group. Do not over commit – be honest with your bandwidth and what you can genuinely accomplish. Most likely, you will only be able to get involved in one or maybe two organizations which is perfectly fine. You'll meet more contacts than you can imagine. The beauty of using this method is that hundreds of industries have associations where members meet to share ideas, build relationships, keep up-to-date on industry trends, and in some cases lobby for common causes. You can go to any search engine, type 'trade association lists' and a number of websites will come up that will give you a comprehensive list or simply type the job title and add association. Once you have identified a few organizations you would like to try out, see if they have a local branch in your city. If they do, you are on your way. Plan to attend the very next event they have. (note: most organizations will allow you to attend a first meeting for free and students should always ask to attend for free or see if there is a reduced rate for students.)

Alumni are a great resource for potential contacts. There are two ways to do this effectively. First, if you live in the same city where you attended a large public university, connecting on the premise that you are both from the same school may not be enough of a link for a meeting since there are thousands just like you. If this is the case, make an effort to get involved in the university's alumni association, perhaps volunteering to serve on a specific committee or simply being consistent in attending class events. If your school is smaller or you attended school out of the state where you live, the ability to leverage alumni connections is easier. The smaller number creates a camaraderie and willingness to meet and help fellow graduates. I have had hundreds of students and clients who have taken advantage of this to great success. A simple e-mail saying you received their name from the alumni office and would like to meet is all you will need to do and the percentages are high that you will receive a positive response. Personally, I have been a great beneficiary of tapping in to my alumni network. When I first arrived in Seattle, I was doing temp work for a dot.com that involved researching the financial planner industry and drafting a needs analysis. I had only been in Seattle for a few weeks so was happy to land the job and enjoyed it, even though the pay was $11.00 per hour. My goal was to get into business development and there happened to be a University of Connecticut graduate, my alma mater, who was leading the business development efforts for a website catering to small firm lawyers. We met and because of the university connection, we immediately hit it off. We were 30 years apart in age, did not know any of the same people, did not have a similar experience in school, but had a bond that proved sufficient enough to establish rapport and build trust. Within two weeks of our meeting, Steve, who is now my mentor and very good friend offered me a job and provided an opportunity for me to use my skills and thrive. It was the break I needed and it would have never happened had I not had the school connection.

Of course, networking events are another good way to identify contacts. We'll talk about how to succeed at networking events beginning with Tip #28, but the key to remember in developing additional contacts is do to four things.

1. Have a clear goal of how many people you want to meet. Events can be difficult for even the most extraverted person so don't kill yourself. Set your goal of how many people you want to connect with and once you achieve it, feel free to leave the event or spend time conversing with already established contacts or friends. It is important to have an achievable goal and once reached, celebrate the result.

2. Write something down immediately after the conversation. You will meet with many people at events and unfortunately, the discussions all end up running together and differentiating one from another becomes difficult. Memorializing a conversation can seem a bit awkward when attending an event so what I recommend is after every few conversations send an e-mail or text to yourself with the person's name and a few topics of each conversation that will spark your memory. We are always checking our phones and

sending messages, so this will seem completely normal and will give you a good break to absorb the discussions you've had and make sure you get the most value from each one.

3. After doing the hard work of successfully connecting with someone at an event, you do not want to lose the momentum. As mentioned in Tip #7, follow up the very next day. This is non-negotiable. Adhere to this practice and it will reap great benefits. Most people simply will not do it. Take the bull by the horns and cement a solid conversation into a potential contact; guaranteeing your hard work will not be for naught. As you are learning from every tip in this book, there is a methodical approach to building strong, trusting, enduring professional relationships – **the key is to follow the system**.

4. The fourth and final step is to take the initial short conversation and try to set up a short meeting or coffee. Try to do this within a month of the first meeting, but make 'the ask' in the e-mail you send the next day. You will still be fresh in the person's mind and having three (event, follow up e-mail, and meeting) touches in the first month will solidify the relationship. It may take a few weeks to set up, that's ok. Stay with it.

Tip #15: Interview professionals for an article you're writing

We will talk about how to get published later in the book, but in conjunction with getting published, this is a good tip to build relationships with industry experts. If you contact people and say you are working on an article and would like 15 minutes of their time to interview them about their thoughts on a specific topic; not too many of them will say no. They may want to confirm your credibility, so do your due diligence and have a great topic for an article or have a good idea where you plan to submit the article for publication. If you've done a good job of preparation, most will make time for the interview. This will provide an opportunity to have an in depth, albeit short, conversation with someone and also gives a very easy excuse to stay in touch. You can update them on the article, tell them when it will be published, and then send a copy of the article with a thank you note once it is published (this technique can be used for old-fashioned print, but also with an online newsletter, or blog post). You will have earned a fan and someone that will want to help you as you seek to take your career to the next level. You will have also helped them get free press and showcase their expertise in the marketplace.

Tip #16: Volunteer

A great way to serve your community and develop relationships with like-minded people is to volunteer. There are so many opportunities in every community to get involved. Choose an organization with a cause that you are passionate about and the tangential benefit will be that you will form strong, enduring relationships. Take your time in choosing where you want to commit your time. Maybe volunteer at a few organizations to start and see what may be the best fit and talk to the executive director and other members of the organization to learn more about their mission. When you have chosen the organization, volunteer with gusto. The key is to volunteer on a consistent basis. You'll feel good about contributing to the community and before you know it, you will have built solid relationships with the other volunteers, members of the board of directors, and many others.

Tip #17: LinkedIn is a Powerful Resource

We all know LinkedIn and have heard about the power of using it, well it is all TRUE. LinkedIn can be a powerful resource to connect with people and maintain contacts. It is also how recruiters at an increasing number of companies identify qualified employees and leads. It is critically important to build contacts on LinkedIn and it's a great way to stay connected to people. There are six keys to differentiate yourself from the average LinkedIn user.
   1. At the top of your profile you have an opportunity to describe who you are professionally. Really give it some thought – recruiters will search for specific keywords and this title could help you pop up more often. It also gives all of your contacts as well as contacts of contacts a way to quickly get a

sense of what you do, without digging too deep into your education or work experience.

2. In addition to your resume, make sure you create a compelling summary of your background and experience – essentially your pitch in a couple of paragraphs. As part of the summary, there is a separate section for you to add specialties. Add as many key words as possible that describe in a word or two your comprehensive experience. This does does need to be full sentences, simply list key words and separate them out with spaces or dashes.

3. Get recommendations. They give you credibility to potential contacts.

4. When inviting someone to connect, always use a personalized note, the generic one provided as a default is not that effective.

5. Join groups and be active. There are hundreds of groups to join and it's an easy way to connect with people in a specific industry. Try to be active by commenting in these forums.

6. Utilize the advanced people search feature to connect with contacts who may be one or two people removed from you.

The Great Conversationalist

Tip #18: Tell A Good Story

Effective conversations are all about exchanging stories. These are not long, drawn out novels, but short, succinct, and specific enough so someone can relate to what you're saying. Whether you are drafting a first paragraph of a cover letter, answering the dreaded 'tell me about yourself' interview question, or connecting with someone at an event or during an informational interview; telling effective stories will be the catalyst to whether you make it to the next step in the relationship. In order to create common ground and truly relate, you have to be specific enough to bring the person into the story, allowing him or her the opportunity to relate. Everyone is capable of telling a great story, it takes practice and the following four tips will help.

1. **Know your audience.** You cannot create common ground or relate to someone if you have no knowledge of their background. Think about your career or personal/professional interests and how certain experiences may particularly resonate with your audience. If you are attending an event about real estate development in Omaha, Nebraska, have at your finger-tips stories that are relatable to the people you may meet. This doesn't have to be a personal story, it could be about an article you read or something you have noticed in the community, or it could be about a personal or work related experience. You cannot do this if you do not know your audience.

2. **Prepare and practice.** Once you know your audience, start preparing for the event by thinking about how you may be able to connect to this individual or group. Think about all the possible experiences or knowledge you may be able to share. Practice **out-loud**, putting your experiences into story format (see a good example of an elevator pitch below). Always, always, always practice out loud. You need to get used to saying the words and practicing out-loud helps you be more conversational. Remember, practice, but do not memorize! If you are sharing a work related experience, you

can use a method that is standard for formal interviews called STAR – Situation, Task, Action, Result. Provide a brief background of the situation with enough detail to connect with the listener, the issue that you needed to solve, the steps you took to solve the problem (making it a story with characters and telling it in a conversational tone), and then explain the result. The STAR method helps keep the story on point and organized. To reiterate, the devil is in the details. Describe the event with specificity.

3. **Pacing is extremely important.** You want to avoid regurgitating information, but instead have a conversation. Think about sharing a cup of coffee at Starbucks with a good friend or family member and exchanging stories. That is the tone and conversational delivery that you must have when connecting with anyone. Most people tend to talk too fast especially when they get nervous so slow down and set the scene.

4. **Be yourself.** In early 2012, I along with another person, Dustin, did a three hour seminar on cross-cultural communication. Dustin began the seminar and was absolutely amazing. He quickly engaged everyone in the audience, challenging them yet also encouraging them to express their views. The energy in the room was incredible and as I was sitting in the corner waiting for my turn, I began getting nervous to the point where I started sweating. I was wondering how I would be able to follow this guy. What could I do to maintain the energy level, how could I incorporate his ability to so seamlessly interact with the entire audience into my portion of the presentation. The nerves increased exponentially for about 15 minutes until I started doing a bit of self-talk. I knew I was a good presenter and I had prepared – I needed to be myself, to have my own style, and that would be the only way I would succeed. After another 10 minutes, my turn came and I stayed true to who I was and my portion of the presentation worked out quite well. Everyone brings something unique to the table that no one else does. No matter what the event or meeting, if you leave it saying the people you met genuinely got to know you; then you have succeeded. Be yourself!

Tip #19: Ask Great Questions: Here are 10 to get you started

When meeting people or going to an association event for the first time, it's always best to learn as much as you can. Open ended questions are the key. Avoid at all costs the 'yes' or 'no' type questions, there is no faster way to have dead air than a close ended question with a one word response. Many conversations will flow from the context of the discussion, so use the following questions to spark ideas or as a way to weave a question into the context of a conversation. Remember, it is not an inquisition and one way to avoid the feeling that it is, is to preface questions with an opinion, an observation, or a re-phrasing of part of the conversation. The questions below are solid and can be tweaked to apply regardless of industry, but if they are not asked in context or you are not prefacing them with knowledge of the individual, context of the conversation, or something that relates to the event; then they will come off as stale or disingenuous.

1. It seems that you have a done a good job of pushing yourself to reach your goals, what's your secret? When you're dead tired, how do you keep going to get that extra bit of work done?
2. I get the impression that you've had incredible success in your career. Can you recall a moment or a time period when you were able to take it to the next step and achieve great success?
3. Something you said earlier reminded me of a book I'm currently reading, …, what are you reading these days? Any book you can recommend that is a must read?
4. Your business has obviously been a success, how'd you go about building such a solid client base?
5. When you were talking about XYZ, it reminded me of an article I read last week that struck me as odd and I'd like to get your thoughts. It was …
6. You touched upon a lot of different areas of the work you're doing and it obviously takes a diverse skill set, what's been your path? How'd you get to this point?

7. Your company seems ripe for international expansion, what markets have you or are considering entering? (International is such a hot topic that it usually can lead to a fruitful discussion)

8. I'm going to guess you are putting a lot of time in at the office, what are you doing these days to relax? How do you achieve work life balance?

9. How have you balanced what seems like a general need for stability with the necessity of taking risks? What does it take to be a good risk taker? (This question can easily be re-framed based on the context of the discussion.)

10. (Depending on the time of year or situation.) Have any plans over the holidays, for the weekend, any summer plans, what are you doing to get through the winter months?

Tip #20: The Elevator Pitch

No matter where you are connecting with people – at an event, a chance meeting, or during an informational interview; the conversation will ALWAYS come back to a simple question that revolves around, 'what do you want to do or why did you decide to contact me'. That is the time when you need to deliver your elevator pitch and nail it. It's a natural way to talk a bit about your background. Take in to account everything that was discussed in Tip #18. The elevator pitch is not something you regurgitate or something that is canned. You need to tailor it to your audience and it needs to be completely conversational in tone, introducing yourself in a professional manner, but as if you were having a conversation with a friend. The following are a couple of examples and specifics on how to develop an effective pitch.

1. "Why did you decide to contact me?" "Well, first, I think Starbucks is an amazing company and I've followed the growth and more recently how the company had to make tough decisions during the recession and now it seems it have emerged stronger and leaner. Second, I had the chance to read a recent article about the work you've done in expanding the company internationally and how you've been instrumental in designing country specific promotional

campaigns and I simply wanted to learn more about how you developed your career to land in such an ideal job. I have an international background, having lived in Taiwan and China and had the opportunity to get some solid marketing experience at Costco so now I'm looking for my next steps and trying to learn as much as I can from experts in the field of international marketing." Again, being natural is the key, but the only way to truly come across as natural is to practice and rehearse. Feeling confident about what you're saying will make you more natural. The best speakers are good because they practice.

2. Why was the above pitch effective?
   a. It is very tailored to the audience and company, showing substantial due diligence had been conducted.
   b. The pitch linked the background and interests of the person with the work the individual is doing and provided enough specifics to allow for follow up questions. For example, a question about Taiwan or China would be a natural. The pitch is almost like a teaser. You want to set it up so it's natural for the person to ask a follow up and if done well, you know the follow up and have an excellent response. You are now in control of the conversation and guiding it in a direction that most benefits you.
   c. You do not need to throw the kitchen sink into your elevator pitch.

3. Here's one more example to consider that looks at the pitch from a recent graduate's perspective. "Where do your interests lie?" "Well, my dream job would be to be a buyer, similar to you, for Nordstrom's, but I realize that's some ways off for me. I have worked in retail since I was sixteen and besides being a top sales performer, I think I developed a keen eye on fashion trends and what types of styles are attractive to the consumer. So at this point, I am looking for anything that will get me closer to my goal, whether that's as a buyer's assistant, something in the marketing department, or maybe working on displays – a step in the direction that will give me additional knowledge and pertinent experience.

I would, of course, love to hear your suggestions on how that may be done or a path you think would be most advantageous for me." In this example, the person was very specific, yet broad in explaining what she wanted. The individual will have a good sense on how to help should an opportunity arise, but the pitch allowed for additional suggestions and advice.

Tip #21: Small Talk is not innocuous

Answering "fine" to the question, "how are you?" - is a horrible answer. That question is an opportunity to engage, to connect right from the moment of shaking hands. If answered perfunctorily, any conversation will start stilted and forced with dead air as both people try to keep the dialog moving forward. A couple of examples: if you're a student, you might say, you'll be a lot better once finals are over or that you've just turned in a major paper, so you're doing great now. If a professional in the job hunt or working but thinking about next steps, focus on something interesting that may have happened to you that week or plans for the weekend. "I'm doing wonderfully, I went to the Entrepreneurs Club breakfast and heard Jim Sinegal of Costco speak and he was fantastic, have you ever heard him?" The two above examples are easy conversation starters; they will both lead to follow up questions and allow you to potentially exchange a quick laugh or establish common ground which is the key to any successful meeting.

The Informational Interview

Tip #22 The Informational Interview

The need to do informational interviews is blasted from the rafters by anyone who advises on career development success to the point that it has almost become a cliché. But, I cannot argue with the results and I am firmly on the bandwagon regarding the effectiveness of doing informational interviews. It's critically important to do these as a core component of your career development strategy. If you generally do not like going to events, then there is nothing more important than making sure you are planning an informational interview at least once per week. In a nut shell, an informational interview is simply an informal meeting that you have with a professional in an area of interest. The person who asked for the meeting is essentially conducting an interview and is responsible for doing enough preparation to create a positive and engaging conversation.

Why do informational interviews?
1. 85% of all jobs do not get posted! The absolute best way to learn about these jobs is through connecting with professionals and building relationships. It's an opportunity to create an advocate for you so when a job is available; you have a great potential contact. Jobs do come from informational interviews, but the primary reason to do informational interviews is to get information and establish long-term professional relationships. This is an opportunity to pick someone's brain, to learn about an area of interest, and connect in a one-on-one setting with a professional who can guide you in your career development.
2. The more people you meet, the higher probability you have of learning about one of thousands of positions that never get posted.
3. To reiterate, you need to enter into every single one of these encounters with a singular goal and that is to **learn and connect**. If you are blatantly job seeking, you destroy your credibility. But, as mentioned, jobs do arise. I have worked

with thousands of students and professionals who have gone on 10, 20, 50 or even up to 100 informational interviews and have gotten to the point that they were sick of them and found them useless. When they thought they could not possibly do one more, a job opportunity arises. I think you are clued in with the why, now let's focus on the how.

Tip #23: How to effectively conduct an informational interview

Be prepared, be genuine, be a good listener, have good questions, and engage in the conversation. **Preparation** focuses on two aspects:
1. Do your due diligence. Know who this person is, what they generally do, and a good bit about the company he/she works for. You want to come across as genuinely interested and engaged. Preparation is the best way to do that.
2. The second component of preparation is to remember that the conversation will always turn back to you and when it does you want to be prepared, essentially, with your elevator pitch (see tip 20). You can have two or three elevator pitches depending on who you're talking to, but in most cases, you will be answering the question, why are you interested in this field or where would you see yourself fitting in, or what do you bring to the table. There are many variations of that question, but you will generally respond with the same concept – which in a very conversational way shows your passion or interest in a specific field and what you can contribute.

The informational interview is not about job solicitation in any respect (SO NEVER ASK FOR A JOB!!), but great companies are always looking for top people so when you have the opportunity to discuss your background, you need to be ready to promote yourself in the most effective way possible. The other key reason to have an effective elevator pitch (Tip #20) is that someone can't help you if they do not know how to help you. What do I mean by this? If you simply say you are looking for anything that will get you in the door, it will not spark the person's memory or make the person think of you if a specific position does arise – you need to let every person you meet with know that you have the skills and passion to do the job. This point is especially true for newer job seekers. Never say: "I'm still figuring things out" or "I'll take anything". You need to be able to articulate exactly what you bring to the table since the person you are meeting with, especially if they are a decision maker, will always ask themselves the question, "How can this person help our company?" It's important to be broad yet specific. For example, if you are looking for a position in marketing, you do not want to limit yourself to only one aspect of the field, yet you want to be specific enough to show that you have given this a lot of thought and are directed.

Now, what you are probably saying at this point is that I just contradicted what I said at the beginning of this tip, well, … not really. Yes, this is for information and you must honestly and genuinely look at it this way, but as I have stressed, opportunities do arise and the informational interview can potentially provide an opportunity to effectively promote yourself. (Note: You should always bring your resume to an informational interview/meeting. Don't pull it out unless the person asks for it, but you should always have it ready just in case.)

Tip #24: The 50 Best Informational Interview Questions

The informational interview, as opposed to a formal interview, requires the person who set up the appointment to control the meeting. The assumption must be made that at the start of the meeting, the interviewee will simply say, "How can I help you." However, as the meeting progresses, the interviewee most likely will also ask questions of the interviewer's background and interests.

Before I outline specific questions, an important point to remember is if you are meeting in a person's office, always try to quickly look around and see if you can create some common ground based on personal effects. These are short conversation starters, but can provide the catalyst for a successful meeting. I personally have a number of pictures from China in my office and at times people will comment on them. As you can imagine, it often leads to quickly developing rapport. One picture is of a parking lot filled with about

300 bicycles and it usually leads to how China has changed, to my own experience of spending the summer in China riding my bike to work, etc. Keep it professional, don't get too personal, but this can be used to great effect.

The last point that leads to a successful informational interview is to preface questions with knowledge. It takes a seemingly generic question and makes it relevant or much more interesting. So for example, "I was reading your bio on your company website and noticed that you recently gave a lecture on the future of biotechnology in Seattle. Your message was optimistic, but I was wondering your thoughts on what Seattle can do to stop our small, successful bio-techs from being gobbled up by larger pharmaceuticals around the country." Do you see the power in that question? I showed that I did my due diligence, that I knew something about the subject area, and had a pointed question that the interviewee would have to think about. Read the question again without the first part and you'll see that it sounds a bit flat. Sometimes it may be difficult to get a large amount of information on the individual. In that case, be creative. Focus your research on the specific company or industry. Ok, let's go through some questions. **These are in no particular order and I've tried to make them universally appealable whether you are a new grad, someone with limited experience, or a veteran of the work world.** For students or new graduates, the biggest tip I can give in the relationship building process is to use your power as a student or someone with very limited experience to be naïve. You are in a position to not know things, use it to your advantage. These questions are the starting point. When you combine them with knowledge obtained from the conversation as well as your due diligence; you will be able to create a compelling question that leads to fruitful dialog.

1. It seems like you have done a very good job of developing the skills and experience to stay one-step-ahead in a very competitive industry, how have you done it?
2. Is there anything you wished you would have pursued or taken advantage of throughout you career?

3. For someone trying to break into the field or with solid experience, but is having trouble getting to the next level. What do you recommend I could do to differentiate myself?

4. Are there any trade publications or associations that you think are the best? What do you do to stay up to date in the industry?

5. I would like to begin to be perceived as an expert in the industry, what would you recommend I do to build a reputation as someone who knows what she is talking about?

6. I'm currently writing an article on the impact social media has had on small businesses and how they leverage this outlet to expand business in the coming years. Who would you recommend I speak to or interview regarding this subject.

7. What about your position makes you pop out of bed in the morning? Is there anything that makes you want to roll over and hit the snooze button?

8. The financial industry looks to be going through a once in a century change, what do you think the industry will look like in a year from now, five years, ten years?

9. Is there any type of volunteer work you would recommend in order to get experience in the field or connect with professionals doing this type of work?

10. ABC Company has done an amazing job of staying relevant where many of your competitors have failed to innovate, how do you think you have done it?

11. For someone with very limited experience in the field, what one piece of advice would you give me that would help me break in to the industry?

12. Do you think it's necessary to change companies in order to advance?

13. If you had to start your career again, would you choose the same path, why or why not?

14. I hope this question isn't too personal, but have you had to make any sacrifices, both personally and professionally, to succeed in this field and do you think they were worth it. (Be careful with this question regarding the personal nature, but ok to ask if you feel the person is talking about his life inside and outside of work or you feel you've developed a very good connection with the person).

15. What are the main reasons that people do not succeed in this field.
16. I know this question sounds a bit generic and I think I have a sense of your responsibilities, but would you mind sharing with me what a typical day looks like?
17. If I am unable to obtain a position in this field, are there any other similar type jobs that you recommend I pursue?
18. What type of things could I be doing now to prepare me for future developments and trends in this industry?
19. What is a typical career path in this field or organization?
20. Are there any particularly interesting programs (projects/cases etc.) that you are currently working on and could share?
21. Can you share with me some of the more challenging situations you've had to face in your position?
22. Is there a lot of cross group collaboration in the company and industry in general, any good examples come to mind?
23. What have been your greatest accomplishments in this position and career in general, have there been any disappointments that come to mind or that you may be willing to share? (My advice is to keep things positive, but again, if the conversation is going well, learning about disappointments can be telling. Use your discretion).
24. How did you go about acquiring the necessary skills to excel in your position?
25. How did you get this job or what job really was the catalyst in developing such a successful career?
26. I have noticed that your company is unique in many ways (such as …) from its competitors, but what do you think differentiates the company from the pack?
27. As someone who is changing careers, what obstacles do you think I need to overcome to be taken as a serious candidate.
28. If you were looking at a resume from a candidate with no directly relevant experience, what types of things would make you take a second look and say, "hmm, I'd like to learn more about this person."
29. Do you know of anyone who took a similar path to the one I'm trying to take? How did it work out? Would you mind connecting me with this person?

30. If you could have an informational interview with anyone in the field, who would it be and why?
31. I have thought about getting an advanced degree in the evening to gain the requisite knowledge, do you have any advice on whether it would help in the field?
32. I have done a lot of research in to the next step in my career and think I can make a good case for wanting to enter ABC profession, do you think I'm fooling myself?
33. I am willing to take a step back to get the necessary experience in order to take two steps forward, but do you think my current career would help catapult me to the next level?
34. Can you give me a sense of the company culture?
35. I recently attended a lecture on future job prospects in high-tech marketing and the prognosis was pretty grim, your thoughts?
36. I appreciate you volunteering to take a quick look at my resume, in trying to get into a position as a games designer, what transferable skills do you think I bring to the table from my career in marketing?
37. Is there any professional development, training, or national conferences you would recommend I attend?
38. What would you consider utopian as far as work environment, how close is ABC Company to achieving it?
39. Who do you go to for professional and career advice? Is there someone in the industry that you particularly admire or use as a sounding board?
40. What types of professional development have you done recently?
41. Although I've seen some downsizing, there have been a few high fliers in your industry, what do you feel are the growth opportunities in your field, in general?
42. What skills and personal characteristics do you think are needed to thrive in this field?
43. Has the company made any recent changes to improve performance, employee satisfaction, or profitability?
44. I know how busy you are and I thank you for your time once again, it's been enjoyable, but that said, if I had additional

questions, would you mind if I contacted you via e-mail or phone?

45. I have been meeting with quite a few people over the last few months and the one question I always like to ask is what your work philosophy is and if you're willing to share, what your personal philosophy on life is?

46. Was this the profession you always thought you would do? When did you make the decision or was it serendipitous?

47. What is the greatest compliment you have ever received regarding your work?

48. What has been your primary motivation that has helped you achieve success in your career?

49. Do you mind if I ask what the next step is for you in your career trajectory or professional development?

50. As mentioned in the building your contact list chapter, the last question has to be: I am just trying to get a lay of the land, do you know anyone else I can talk to?

Tip #25: The Unsolicited Informational Interview Letter

We have discussed methods to develop a comprehensive contact list, but there will be times when the only way to to initiate a connection is through an unsolicited informational interview letter. This technique is used when there is an important connection to make and you have tried all other methods to create an introduction but have come up empty. A tailored, hard-copy letter can be extremely effective to initiate a connection.

The letter is a creative writing exercise. What can you say in the first paragraph or first couple of sentences that will make the reader want to read on? How can you genuinely catch his or her attention? This takes a lot of time and effort, so perhaps you're asking why do it? Well, the best people are sometimes the hardest to connect with so to truly build a solid network of professionals who are at a point in their career that they can make an impact in your career development, you need to think outside the box. In addition, it can be good that it takes great effort since the harder it is, the less people will do it and you will be at a strategic advantage if you exert the effort and write a compelling letter. If you are intrigued to learn more, let's discuss how to write an impactful letter.

1. The first sentence has to really make the reader sit up and say, I want to know more about this person, I want to read on, hmm, that's interesting. What can you say in the first sentence that will generate that kind of attention? Well, you need to be creative, it needs to be very personal, and you need to make it a story. We connect through the story. We remember the great stories, we love sharing stories, and great leaders inspire through stories. It is very different from a cover letter. You are not saying in the first sentence, "I have 10 years working in high tech marketing and I would enjoy the opportunity to speak with you." Not a bad sentence for a cover letter, but to get in front of a person for an informational interview who doesn't know you, it's going to take a lot more. The first sentence grabs the reader and the rest of the first paragraph tells the rest of the story in a very organized manner – the way I want you to think about this paragraph is to answer the question: what am I passionate about and why.

Tip #26: Creative is the Key to Connection

Following is a paragraph that I worked on with a student at Seattle University that will illustrate the point and led to informational interviews with every real estate development player in Seattle and ultimately a job during the worst real estate crash since the great depression. There was no job available. This person created one by connecting, building relationships, and showing his worth, but it all started with this letter.

"For over three years, I worked in one of the toughest commercial real estate markets in the country, Detroit, Michigan. As a young commercial broker, I faced many challenges in order to find success in a region with soaring vacancy rates and very few completed transactions. During this time my passion for real estate crystallized and I learned that great things can be accomplished with hard work, loyalty and a thirst for knowledge."

That is a very solid first paragraph - it is telling a story in a well written, cogent, succinct style. It is not run of the mill so grabs the reader's attention right from the first sentence. The last sentence of the first paragraph focuses on the ultimate reason for writing the letter. The above is very good or something like, 'I am passionate about this field, but as I take the first steps in my career, I realize I have a great deal to learn.' If you are already in the industry and have knowledge or are thinking of changing careers, you can tweak the above sentence to fit the situation. The last sentence provides a good segway to the next paragraph and the ultimate ask for a meeting.

Let's look at the remainder of this letter.

"I moved to Seattle two years ago after researching a number of cities that I felt could best offer me the opportunities to develop my career and pave the way to reaching my goals. It was at this time that I first learned of Paul Allen's vision for South Lake Union. From the acquisition and assembly of roughly 60 acres, to the completion of the Streetcar, and to the recent deal announced with Amazon; I am genuinely excited watching Vulcan's vision become a reality."

"I am writing to you with a sincere interest of meeting you for a few moments. I am at a cross-road with my career and would like to ask your advice on breaking in to the real estate development and investment industry. While I know you are very busy, just a few moments of your time would be both helpful and engaging."

In the second paragraph, you can see how it is very tailored to the work the person is doing and it shows a genuine interest in and passion for Vulcan's vision.

Put pen to paper and try to be as creative as possible; you'll be surprised at your results. If you write a creatively tailored letter, you will find that the response rate will be quite high.

Tip #27: The follow up to the informational interview letter

From my experience, if you have taken time to really personalize a letter, people are generally keen to help and you will most likely get some bites. For the people that did not respond, it is important to persevere and the best way to do that is with a call. The best time to make a call is late in the day, usually around 4:30 or 5:00 since the person you are trying to contact will likely still be at his/her desk, but the gatekeeper will have gone home. If you get through to the person, give a very brief - who you are, reminder about the letter, and what you want. Most people will probably say ok and set something up. If the person is not there, leave a short succinct message and hopefully they'll get back to you. If after the letter and a phone call, you still have no luck connecting, then try e-mail. After two attempts (letter and phone), the person will probably recognize your name and may respond. If that still does not work and you really want to meet this person, be creative and persistent, but if not, let it go. There are many fish in the sea and you want to stay positive about the process and not get frustrated.   You tried and now move on to the people who do want to connect with you and focus your energy on making those meetings as productive as possible.

Thriving at Events & in Organizations

The Event: How to do it Well

We spent a good deal of time talking about how to find people, the tactics of choosing an organization, and a variety of ways to get that first meeting. Let's now focus our attention on how to thrive at events.

Tip #28: Be Socially Intelligent

There are four characteristics that almost all socially intelligent people possess.

1. **Be Real.** Your very best self will only emerge if you are steadfast in being true to who you are as an individual. Posers are spotted immediately, while those that are genuine, warts and all, will attract many friends and professional allies. Embrace authenticity and attending events will be that much more enjoyable.

2. **Be Curious.** Genuinely attempt to learn about the person. Ask follow up questions and try to connect your own experiences with the person. People are most impressed with thoughtful, insightful questions. Practice the art of the question, using the questions contained in this book as a starting point.

3. **Be conscious of the Interests and Intentions of the Person** This is all about reading and understanding the emotions of the individual. You get much better at this skill with practice and over time will be able to craft your conversation and questions around what you know to be important to the potential contact. To start, simply try to be conscious of the person's facial expressions, tone of their voice, and how they are reacting to the conversation. It will give you clues into what is important and how best to connect in the short-term and keys to building a sustainable relationship in the long-term.

4. **Avoid Negative Self-Talk**

Stay positive and enthusiastic about yourself and the event you are attending. Avoid at all cost going down the slippery slope of negative self-talk. It's extremely easy to do and and may lead to you not attending the event or if you go, having a horrible experience. If you convince yourself that the event will probably be a waste, will likely not help you in your future career, or will be just be another boring gathering of people who you doubt have anything in common with you, you can guess the result. As we have discussed in detail in an earlier tip, there is usually no instant gratification in building relationships, but it is a given that is is critical to do, so in order to make sure you are continuing to develop necessary connections throughout your career, you have to stay engaged and positive with the day-to-day tasks that are essential to long-term career development success.

Tip #29: Preparation

Before attending an event, do your research. The following seven guidelines will ensure you are using your time effectively and are prepared.

1. **Know the organization.** Read the bios of the board of directors, study the website for any recent publicity the organization has had, and make sure you thoroughly understand their mission.
2. **Know the speaker.** Many networking events are combined with short presentations. Research the speaker, know his/her background, and learn as much as you can about the topic. This will provide easy conversation starters as well as make your questions more pointed and intelligent.
3. **Know yourself.** We have discussed this in a previous tip, but make sure to review your pitch, practicing out loud so you come across as naturally as possible.
4. **Know the attendees.** Go the extra mile and learn about the organization's key constituents and what types of professionals usually attend the events. The executive director of the organization may not be able to provide a list of attendees, but will usually be willing to provide a snapshot of who has attended similar events in the past.

5. **Know your questions** (see Tips 19 and 24). Have a list of open ended questions prepared in advance of the event. Conversation will likely flow naturally, but you'll feel much more confident walking in to a room with some solid questions about the organization, speaker, and just general conversation starters.

6. **Know your current events**. Most conversations will start with what's going on in the news. Avoid controversial topics, but prepare to speak about the local sports teams, local economy/companies, movies, and anything else interesting that has happened in the news. It does not need to be a serious discussion; entertainment and the quirky are excellent ice breakers.

7. **Have a follow up strategy**. If you effectively prepare for an event, you most likely will come away with at least five contacts. Make sure you have a method to remember a key piece of information regarding your conversation (e-mail or text yourself or bullets on the back of a business card work well) and send a follow e-mail no later than 24 hours after the event.

Tip #30: Build Trust through Pro-Active Listening

An effective relationship does not exist without trust and a core component of building trust is to be a proactive listener. The following five points will improve your skills dramatically.

1. **Treat the person you are talking to as the most important person in the room.** We are all guilty of scanning the room while talking to someone else; thinking of the next person or supposedly more important person we want to talk to while doing our best to remove ourselves from the current conversation. It's tough not to do, whether we see a friend enter a room or a potential contact that we've been trying to meet, our eyes and thoughts will drift away from the person right in front of us. The master communicators avoid this and have trained themselves to be laser focused on the present, giving their full attention to the current conversation. Politics aside, former President Bill Clinton was the absolute

master at treating every person he met, with a dignity that involved focusing all his attention and energy on the individual he was speaking with. If you do it well, it's unbelievably powerful. Easy to understand but very difficult to do. Be conscious of it.

2. **Do not formulate an answer while you're listening.** This is another point that we are all guilty of. We know we shouldn't do it, but in most cases it becomes unavoidable. Once again, it is something that you need to be conscious of and practice – over time you'll break the habit. Once we start formulating a response, we have drifted from what the person is saying and are more interested in proving we are smart enough to contribute to the topic. STAY PRESENT! You will have plenty of time to make your point or add your interesting anecdote, but truly great connectors and conversationalists have mastered the technique of listening to the words being said and formulating a response after the person has finished speaking.

3. **Have the confidence to not provide the answer.** It has happened to all of us. The little voice inside our head is saying, unless we show we are smart, we will not come across as credible. In fact, credibility is always established through genuine understanding of the issue which cannot be obtained unless you are listening intently and asking effective follow up questions. Get away from the habit of only thinking you can provide insight through sharing your wisdom. Most decision makers will say an excellent set of follow up questions showing genuine understanding of the problem is the most effective way to establish credibility and respect.

4. **Paraphrase.** Show that you are listening by restating what you've heard and then allowing the person to continue.

5. **Body language is important.** Show that you are engaged non-verbally. Lean in to the conversation, don't have your arms crossed, have strong eye-contact, acknowledge through occasional nods and smiles.

Tip #31: The Name Game

We all already know how important this is, but most of us are not good at it and we think it's ok to just say hello, good to see you again. IT IS NOT! Whether they say it or not, people recognize that you have remembered their name and I have seen on many occasions how a conversation that starts with, "good to see you again, Shawn" has more energy and pop to it. There are a number of simple techniques. To help people remember your name, see if you can provide an easy association that will stick in someone's mind. For me, I always say Shawn Lipton, Lipton like the tea. What happens quite often is that when I run into someone again, they usually will say, "I know Lipton, like the tea, but what was your first name again." More ideal to have some sort of link to your first name, but you get the idea. Another good technique is to repeat your first name twice. "Shawn, Shawn Lipton." It will stick just a bit more deeply. To remember someone else's name, first make sure you are present when meeting them, don't think about what you'll say (you already know your name), stay focused on the other person's name and repeat it: I'm Bill Dixon, Hi Bill, nice to meet you. That will help. If you can, try to make an introduction for Bill and use his name again. If you have a moment alone, try to repeat the names of the people you have been introduced to and try to visualize their face and connect with the name. Say the name a couple of times to yourself with the visualization of the person's face. These techniques will all help. Finally, before attending an event, try to go through your database and review all the names of the contacts that you have made at previous events for this group. The simple tactic of remembering names will leave a strong impression with everyone you meet.

Tip #32: Show up Early

This tip is so absolutely simple, but five years from now, if you only remember one thing from this book, make it tip number 32. This has worked for me on so many occasions and for so many of my clients that I can't understand why the majority of people still think it's good practice to arrive fashionably late. Personally, at an event when I arrive late, I almost feel like I'm intruding. Most people are already having conversations, the food has been picked over, and the line to get a drink is long. There's just no way to be on your A game and really use the event for its intended purpose if you show up late.

On the other hand, when I show up early, I always feel like I am one of the hosts of the event. I usually stand pretty close to the registration table greeting people as they enter and before I know it, I've met 10 or 15 folks. The early birds also have something in common, they are there EARLY!! Arriving early allows for an easy conversation starter since for all of the early arrivers, there is no one else to talk to besides a few people. As the event fills up and you are walking around the room, you'll see many familiar faces and if they happen to be speaking in a group or with someone you've targeted that you would like to meet, it becomes much easier to approach and say, "May I join you". (Note: if you ask to join a conversation, be gracious. It may be appropriate to introduce yourself, but then insist on not interrupting the on-going conversation.) **This works for all other types of gatherings – if you're going to a seminar, an association meeting, a sporting event; show up early!** Going to these types of programs takes time out of your busy work day or your personal life, so make sure you leverage the event to its fullest. There is nothing worse than coming home from a program and saying to yourself, "what a waste of time". Showing up early will help you avoid ever having to say that.

Tip #33: Be Consistent

As we discussed earlier, the most successful method to build strong relationships is through the soft sell, thus the need to be consistent. One of the best networkers I ever met was passionate about technology so he joined the Technology Entrepreneurs Club. Every month, he would go to the meeting. No matter what else was going on, it was a have-to-have in his mind and his goal was just to connect, to contribute to the conversation, and volunteer when needed. Slowly, people started to get to know and like him. He did this over a two year period and overtime, he started to generate business for his company and his next job was a direct result of a relationship he built at the club. He initially started going to meetings to meet like-minded people and to establish professional relationships with colleagues in the community – he was not looking for business or for a new position. It happened organically. This will not happen if you only show up occasionally or if you don't commit to getting involved. This takes time and major effort so be honest with your time commitments and what you are able to accomplish.

Speaking & Publishing: Become an Expert

One way to build credibility in a field, increase your base of contacts, and become an expert is to start a blog. A well written blog gets noticed. If you're writing about a topic that you're passionate about, you'll slowly begin to build a following. It's uncanny how many searches I've done for information and landed on a blog post from a random person who has written about the exact topic that interests me. That post lives on and continues to attract a following. Some of the best blog posts are lists – top five interviewing techniques, best books about China, 10 free ways to market your business. You get the picture. A blog is still one of the best ways to attract an audience, build relationships, and show your expertise in a specific field. The key is to be consistent. A podcast is another way to build a following.

In addition to creating a blog or podcast, getting published in print or online publications is easier than you might imagine. People just like you get published all the time. The following tip provides some first steps on identifying potential topics and publications.

Tip #34: Finding a topic and identifying publications

To find a topic that you think has the potential for getting published, do your research, interview experts in the field, know your audience, and identify publications.

1. **Use your Knowledge.** It is going to be pretty difficult to motivate yourself to write if you are starting completely from scratch. Take a topic that you are passionate about and start doing your research. Find articles online, in magazines, books – absorb all the information you can and then from there try to identify gaps, topics that have yet to be written about that might be informative. Blend topics together. Based on all of your research and reading, see if you can think creatively on how a variety of topics relate, thus developing a completely new idea. Use mentors, colleagues, and others you respect as sounding boards – brainstorm with

them to refine your topic and approach and then put pen to paper.

2. **Interview Subject Matter Experts.** An excellent approach to building relationships and to get published is to interview subject matter experts. It provides an easy way to connect with people since most won't turn down an opportunity to show their expertise and will be flattered with the request. It's also a bit of an easier method then coming up with a completely new piece of work and may be a perfect baby-step. Take the time to identify a topic and interview five to ten experts in the field and from those interviews, craft a compelling article.

3. **Identify Publications.** The best place to start is with industry publications, whether online or print. Generally industry focused publications are more amenable to unpublished authors and if you have done your due diligence and have identified a compelling topic, your likelihood of getting published increases dramatically.

4. **Know your audience.** Be conscious of your target audience and their interests. The most artfully written prose is meaningless if nobody wants to read it. As part of your research, think about what topics would appeal to your target market that are currently not getting addressed.

Tip #35: Help a Reporter

www.helpareporter.com is an amazing site to build your reputation as an expert. The site is free and it connects journalists who are looking for information on specific topics with subject matter experts who may have the background or knowledge that would be valuable for the journalist. As you are developing your reputation in a field and trying to build relationships with key decision makers, your ability to create a presence in that field by getting quoted in articles can be extremely effective. This site is the perfect catalyst to make that happen.

Tip #36: Make a presentation

The beauty of spending the time to publish is that is gives you the content to make a presentation - another amazing way to build an effective network and get recognized as an expert. To start, I would base it on the article that you have written for publication. It is not important if it has been published when you start approaching organizations to speak at their events. It would help, but the key is that you have a compelling topic and feel confident in your knowledge on the subject matter. Believe it or not, there are always organizations looking for speakers – every major city has hundreds of organizations that meet on a monthly basis and generally are looking for speakers on a variety of topics. It could be the Marketing Association of San Francisco, The Rotary, Washington Software Alliance, a foreign travel club, or a meet-up group. If you have a story to tell and have come up with a unique or hot topic, the only thing holding you back is your ability to take a risk and go for it.

Keeping in Touch

Tip #37: It is Easier to Make than Maintain a Relationship

It has happened to all of us. We meet someone great, have an amazing conversation, exchange business cards, perhaps we even send a thank you e-mail or card saying how nice it was to meet the person. It is someone you definitely want to keep in touch with, cultivate a relationship with, and if all goes as planned, this person could possibly be someone who could provide a future opportunity whether as a business partner, a new job, or a friend. A valuable relationship is in the making. BUT, time passes, perhaps six months or a year and you realize that this great potential relationship is dead. This may not be a big deal; however, it is usually when you need the connection that you realize that it has been lost. Perhaps you need their expertise or maybe you've identified a position at their company that you'd like to apply for or maybe you want to introduce a colleague to this person, thus doing a good job of being a connector, but you did not keep in touch and since you didn't keep in touch, it becomes more difficult to reach out and actually ask for something.

Yes, you could still try and if you get lucky, the person will respond, but the more likely scenario is that your great contact will say, "who is this guy, I met him a year ago, he didn't keep in touch and now, out of the blue, he wants something". DELETE! Your e-mail joins the delete folder abyss. MAINTAIN, MAINTAIN, MAINTAIN! The best relationships builders are the one's who are methodical about keeping in touch. Have an excellent contact management system (there are many good, inexpensive ones; I use batchbook.com) and set aside time each week to update it. Have ticklers connected to Outlook that remind you to reconnect. The truly great networkers are not the individuals who know how to work a room, but those that have mastered the art of relationship maintenance.

Tip #38: Be Methodical

Excellent record keeping is essential! In addition to the basic contact information, detail how you met each person. Just one sentence of the initial connection – whether another person introduced you, met at an event, someone who had been following you on Twitter, etc. Just one sentence that will help you remember the contact. Another key data point is to write down every time you have connected with the person and a sentence of what transpired. Maybe you connected at an event, or sent a holiday card, or forwarded an interesting article, or suggested an opportunity for this person to get some free press. Whatever the case, memorialize the action and the date in your database. Maintaining and building relationships is connecting two or three times per year, so you want the last time you connected with a specific person staring you in the face every time you open their profile. It's a reminder and may provide a bit of recourse or accountability when you fall off the wagon. If it's been six months, you know you need to find a way to connect and push yourself to reach out (see Tip #40 below).

In addition to the above tips, ideally you'll also want to provide specifics of each conversation. You will connect with a lot of people and in many cases the same topics arise. In a matter of weeks, it is possible you will have completely forgotten about what you have discussed with any particular person. You do not need to regurgitate the entire conversation, but do be specific and provide essential details. It doesn't have to be professional, it can be about an upcoming vacation that the person spoke to you about, names of kids, good restaurants etc. This goes an incredibly long way in building a strong relationship and setting the stage for your next conversation or e-mail. I cannot stress this point enough – it has worked wonders for me.

Tip #39: Keep in touch when you don't need to

The key to building a mutually beneficial relationship is to show you care about the relationship by keeping in touch when you don't need to. If you wait until you do need the contact, it is too late. It is what I like to call the Soft Sell of networking. You build the relationship over time and then if there ever comes a time when you need to ask for something, YOU CAN! Remember, you need to genuinely be interested in building these relationships; you need to value this person as a professional colleague and not look at this connection as opportunistic. Always think if there is any way you can help or provide value. Do opportunities and planned happenstance arise from having built a solid network of contacts? Absolutely! But, never think about a relationship in terms of what's in it for me. Once you have established the credibility, that person will bend over backwards to do what they can to help – not because they feel obligated, but because they want to support a professional friend, someone they have gotten to know, respect and someone they want to see succeed. Contacts will want to genuinely help and will look for nothing in return because you established the connection and made a major effort when you didn't need to and weren't looking for anything.

Tip #40: How do I keep in touch

I know, it is easy to say, keep in touch, keep in touch, keep in touch! But how?? What if you have nothing to say, no more questions to ask, what can you do to keep in touch? Following are some of the methods that work.

1. **Milestones in your life or theirs.** This is a fantastic method. First, a milestone in your professional life is an ideal way to reconnect. If you have started a new position, gotten a promotion, taken on new responsibilities, have become a board member of an organization; let your contacts know. You may have a LinkedIn account and I encourage you to use it and update your profile. This is a great way to stay connected and your contacts will receive updates on things occurring in your professional life, but it is not enough and a bit too passive. Do not send a broadcast e-mail. Send individual e-mails of just a couple of sentences giving a brief update on your milestone. "Dear Bill, I wanted to let you know that I have taken a new position at my company focusing on strategic partnerships with Original Equipment Manufacturers. I'm excited about the prospects of getting to the next level of my career. I wanted to make sure to tell you

since during our informational interview, we had discussed a similar move you made early in your career. I look forward to keeping in touch. Regards, Shawn." You can't even imagine how many responses you'll receive congratulating you and wishing you the best in your new endeavor. This method also works for milestones in someone else's life. LinkedIn is the best way to track this. You'll get updates when your contacts change their profiles. Comb through those on a consistent basis and e-mail folks notes of congratulations. In addition to LinkedIn, you may read something in the paper, see an update on a company website, or hear some news through the grapevine. This is an ideal way to reach out. "Dear Sarah, I saw you quoted in the Puget Sound Business Journal last week, interesting article, congrats. Hope all is well. Regards, Shawn." I'll guarantee you'll get a nice response thanking you for the kudos and for noticing. It takes very little time, but very few people do it since it requires excellent follow up and organization. To emphasize, LinkedIn makes your networking efforts amazingly efficient. The other day, I was looking through updates of my contacts and noticed an attorney I knew had just been promoted to partner. I sent her a quick e-mail congratulating her. By the end of the day she had responded.

2. **Sending an article.** Another great method of keeping in touch is by sending an article. People will greatly appreciate that you made the effort and will usually respond quite quickly thanking you for thinking of them. I do this all the time and people also send me articles on a frequent basis. This method works so well because we generally want to stay up to speed on areas of interest, but we are all busy and do not have time to read every news source. I first realized the importance of this method years ago when I was trying to maintain contact with a labor law attorney. I had been reading an article in Business Week Online that a number of Starbucks stores in New York City were trying to unionize. I immediately thought of the attorney and sent her the link to the article. I kept it short and sweet. "Dear Emily, I hope all is going well. I just read this article on Starbucks employees trying to unionize and I thought you may be interested in

reading it. Keep in touch. Regards, Shawn." Within ten minutes I got a response thanking me for thinking of her, saying she had not read it, but was very interested in the subject. From then on, I was hooked. As I sent articles to people, they in kind would return the favor, thus really cementing our relationship. Use this technique sparingly, once or twice a year – you don't want flood a person's inbox.

3. **Sending holiday cards** is an excellent way to keep in touch. I send out hundreds of personalized *(they must be personalized with at least one or two sentences)* cards each year and the responses I receive thanking me for the card is really quite amazing. As with any relationship building technique, this has to be genuine. You want to wish someone well during the holiday season and the coming year and it cannot be opportunistic. If you are genuine, the card will resonate. The other point to re-emphasize is that these need to be personalized, and not the generic signature or stamp. The message does not need to be long, but it MUST be tailored to each individual.

4. **Thank someone for their advice.** If you had a great meeting with someone and took their advice at some point down the road, let them know. They will appreciate you taking the time to send the e-mail.

Tip #41: Be a Connector and Serve Your Network

The very best networkers are the best connectors. They are always trying to think of how to bring people together. This could be for potential business, a mentor with a mentee, an informational interview, or a potential job lead. To be effective in building a solid base of professional relationships, it is absolutely essential to PAY IT FORWARD! You don't just want to take, you want to give back and the ideal way to do that is to always be thinking about and on the look-out for how you can connect people within your network. It's easy to do, once you do it a few times and get on a role. Give more than you get – try to help as much as you can.

Tip #42: Subscribe to www.helpareporter.com

In Tip #35, I spoke about this site as an ideal place to begin to promote yourself as an expert, but it is also one of the best ways to effectively help your contacts and serve the people in your network. By subscribing to this website, you will get e-mails with queries from journalists who are working on specific stories and need experts to comment on the story. The site connects journalists, authors, and bloggers with subject matter experts in a variety of fields and provides an ideal way for people to build a reputation as an expert. Subscribe to their e-mail and if you see a request from a journalist that one of your contacts might be interested in; send them an e-mail. It is a great way to serve your network and maintain the connection.

Tip #43: The Thank you Card

After any meeting you have with someone, always send a thank you e-mail. Keep it short; focusing on something you spoke about and thank the person for taking the time. You will usually get a response saying how much they enjoyed meeting you and volunteering to help in any way they can. What this e-mail is saying is that you want to make the extra effort to thank someone and the meeting was important to you.

<u>Your Plan of Action</u> (After Tip #50 is a sample plan)

Tip #44: The simpler the better

Your plan should be no more than one or two pages and needs to be a living breathing document. Something you go back to on a day-to-day basis to update and confirm that you are following through. Much like a resume, you should be able to scan your networking plan in about 10 seconds and be able to see the type of progress you're making. It should not be burdensome to create – this can be done in a couple of hours. Many of you may be thinking that you want to just get to it and not worry about the plan, but taking the time to have something in writing and organized will pay off with huge dividends. This cannot be a nice-to-have in your career development strategy; **it is a have-to-have.** You must memorialize your strategy to make it real and to have the accountability you need to follow through with action.

The key is to be honest with the amount of time you are able to commit. One informational interview per week will work for some of you, but others will want to do two or three. Some of you will spend an hour per week researching industry trends, some of you can do much more. Some will write an article in six months, others may be able to write a book in that amount of time. Be consistent, persevere, and commit.

Tip #45: Summarize the reasons why you are networking

There has to be a compelling reason why you are undertaking the effort to connect with people and build relationships. If you don't have this type of driver, it will be easy to blow-off an event, not spend the time to have informational interviews, and not attend to the sometime tedious task of maintaining all of your contacts and keeping good records. As we have discussed throughout this book, building relationships is a soft-sell, it's a process that takes time - delayed gratification is the key. Motivation can be difficult since there is no urgency like an impending deadline or upcoming interview; it's important to create the urgency by keying in on the direct benefits.

Tip #46: Write down your commitment for the week

Keep it simple. At the top of a page, write down a one or two sentence commitment. This may or may not change week-to-week. It's important to be able to look at this sheet of paper and your planned networking activities for the week and see the reason, in a one or two sentence summary, of why you are putting in this effort. The commitment should also be motivating. The commitment can be anything you want. It can be as simple as, 'focus on one task per day, get it done, and celebrate the accomplishment,' or 'commit to 45 minutes per day, every day and celebrate with a massage at the end of the week,' or "find your passion, live your life to the fullest, and celebrate each victory,' or "each of these goals takes me closer to finding my dream career,' or it could be a favorite quote that provides the motivation and commitment to push through and achieve your goals for the week such as my favorite Goethe quote mentioned in a previous tip. Whatever you choose, make it meaningful, create a sense of urgency, and don't forget to celebrate the victories.

Tip #47: Chunk your goals and set time aside each day

We discussed this in great detail under the accountability section (Tips #1-6), but it's worth reiterating. As we all know and have discussed, networking is hard work. To do it consistently, **it is necessary to set small, weekly, achievable goals.** Do not write it down unless you think you can accomplish the task that week. Be that steadfast in your networking plan of action. Writing something down, means it will get done. There will be times when you have over estimated and just cannot accomplish one of your goals for the week, that's ok. Do not beat yourself up over it, but you must look at your one page weekly plan as so important, that nothing gets written on it unless it will be done. I'd rather see short and doable, than the kitchen sink with most goals left undone.

Tip #48: Have a long term plan of action

Attached to your weekly plan, it's important to have a one page six month plan. There should be one or two sentences that describe, in detail, a long range goal that you can look at on a daily basis and see something concrete, something to work toward. The second portion of the long range plan should simply be a list of 10 bullets that you would like to accomplish over the next six months: tasks, strategies, projects, and meetings that you need to do, but will take significantly more time than a week. This list can be a bit more fluid. Projects may be added and deleted depending on a variety of circumstances, including how your career development plan is progressing on a weekly basis and any new directions you wish to take. BUT, at the end of the six months, 10 bullets need to have been brought to fruition. There cannot be any negotiation here.

The weekly plan as well as the six month plan needs to be shared with your accountability partner.

Tip #49: Have a list of contacts

In your weekly plan, you want to have a list of people you plan to connect with during that week, whether it's a meeting that has already been set up or it's someone that you need to follow up with so you stay on their radar or it's someone you are contacting for the first time. This is the core of your weekly plan and will keep you focused on what you need to do to succeed. You want to write those names down and after you connect, to check off the done box next to that goal. It will feel good, keep you focused, and on task.

Tip #50: State why you are connecting and how you will connect

With every contact you have, state the reason why you are connecting with that person and what you want to accomplish in the meeting. This should not be more than one or two sentences. Succinct and to the point, but every single contact you make should have a specific purpose. It could be as simple as – 'need information, top person in field' or a bit more detailed – 'want to work for this company, this person is a small first step to learning about the organization and how I may be able to position myself'.

Nothing more than that is necessary. This also helps when prioritizing your contact list. Having a one or two sentence reason why you need to connect with someone will help clarify who should be at the top of list and where extra effort should be placed.

Date

Commitments

1.

2.

3.

Goals and Execution Plan

Goal	Execution Plan	Completion Date	Result

People to Connect with:

Name	E-mail	Phone
1.		
2.		
3.		

Long-Term Goal

1.

Sample E-Mail

Subject line: Read your article

Dear Mr. Sparks:

I recently read your article in the Puget Sound Business Journal on formulating a successful international marketing strategy. My name is Shawn Lipton and I have been on the business development side of the business for five years which involved an 18 month assignment in China and am now looking to jump to marketing. In the article, you mentioned that your career took a variety of twists and turns before you landed in your dream job of international marketing. As I take the next steps in my career, I was wondering if you could spare 15 minutes of your time to allow me to pick your brain.

I would very much appreciate your insight and advice.

Best regards,
Shawn

Your Dream Job Awaits

We all know passively applying for jobs online for the majority of job seekers is useless. Millions of people do it every day and sit back waiting for their dream job to hop in their lap and say, "here I am". Why do people continue to do it if it is so unsuccessful? It's easy, requiring little effort and it makes us feel like we are at least doing something. Relationship building, on the other hand, is hard work. It can be uncomfortable and lead to awkward conversations, a feeling that you've wasted your time, and when starting the process, a hit to your self-esteem. But, it works and in the thousands of people I have coached, the ones that pushed through the initial discomfort, realized that networking is an easily learned skill, even for introverts, and that the short and long term benefits greatly outweighed the initial blows to the ego. I challenge you to expose yourself to potential failure, to rejection, to the possibility of having a negative experience at an event, and stick with it. If you do, you will realize the power of relationship building, you'll kick yourself for not starting the process earlier, and you'll yield tremendous benefit, leading to incredible career success and fulfillment. Indeed, your dream job awaits!

About the Author

Shawn Lipton has been advising students and professionals about how to effectively network for the last seven years. He has coached thousands of individuals in developing effective strategies and the requisite motivation to land their ideal job through building long-standing, mutually beneficial, trusting relationships. Prior to starting his own company, The Trusted Coach (www.thetrustedcoach.com) and serving as assistant dean of the Center for Professional Development at the Seattle University School of Law, Shawn spent considerable time in China and Taiwan working, studying, and traveling throughout Asia. He speaks Mandarin Chinese fluently. Shawn is also the author of a spy novel, *China's Master Plan*.